COSY EASTER

CUTE & COSY COLOURING BOOK

Amelia Green

A LITTLE NOTE FROM AMELIA GREEN

Thank you so much for choosing this colouring book!
I hope it brings you a moment of calm, creativity, and joy.

Curious how we colour the pages or looking for fresh ideas?
Come hang out on TikTok and Instagram.

tiktok.com/@AmeliaGreenColoring
instagram.com/AmeliaGreenColoring

If you'd like to show us your coloured pages,
post a pic or video and tag us.

Now grab your favourite pens, get comfy, and let's make the world a little more colourful, one page at a time!

COLOUR TEST PAGE

This book is printed on quality paper, but if you use alcohol-based markers, we recommend that you insert a sheet behind the page to protect subsequent pages.

Happy
Easter

HAPPY EASTER

HAPPY
EASTER

HAPPY
EASTER

EASTER
STORIES

EASTER
GIFT
DELIVERY

FINISH

1

EASTER
SALE

PENGUIN BOOKS

UK | USA | Canada | Ireland | Australia
India | New Zealand | South Africa | China

Penguin Random House Australia is part of the Penguin Random House group of companies whose addresses can be found at global.penguinrandomhouse.com.

First published by Penguin, an imprint of Penguin Random House Australia Pty Ltd, in 2026

Printed and bound in Australia by Griffin Press, an accredited ISO AS/NZS 14001 Environmental Management Systems printer

A catalogue record for this book is available from the National Library of Australia

ISBN 978 1 76135 987 3 (Paperback)

penguin.com.au

We at Penguin Random House Australia acknowledge that Aboriginal and Torres Strait Islander peoples are the Traditional Custodians and the first storytellers of the lands on which we live and work. We honour Aboriginal and Torres Strait Islander peoples' continuous connection to Country, waters, skies and communities. We celebrate Aboriginal and Torres Strait Islander stories, traditions and living cultures; and we pay our respects to Elders past and present.